Fly With Me

by Claudette Cleveland

Fly With Me
by Claudette Cleveland

Copyright © July, 1998 by Claudette Cleveland

Published and distributed in the United States by

White Star Enterprises
P.O.Box 217
O"Fallon, IL, 62269
618-277-7247

All rights reserved. No part of the book may be reproduced by any mechanical, photographic, or electronic process, or in the form of a phonographic recording, nor may it be stored in a retrival system, transmitted, or otherwise be copied for public or private use--other than for :fair use: as brief quotations embodied in articles and reviews without prior written permission of the publisher.

First Printing July, 1998

Cover Painting
Title: **Flight**
Watercolor by Claudette Cleveland

Contents

Introduction	5
Fly With Me	8
I Fired Doubting Thomas	14
Nature Beings	17
Forces of Nature	23
The Crow	29
What's A Crystal	35
The Butterfly	38
Lake Titicaca	41
The Reed People	47
Machu Picchu	49
Sedona	54
The Wizard	61
Transformation	63
So Familiar	66
Who Is Cassandra	69
Becoming A Member Of The Cast	72
The New Zealand Maori	74
Milarepa	80
Her Eyes, The Window To Her Soul	86
The Lotus	89
Bamboo	90
No Beginning, No End	94
Author's Biography	96

We dedicate this book to all the seekers of truth.
&
Of course all the friends who encouraged and supported this venture.

Introduction

While in college as an art student, I found that if I went to sleep for an hour or so, I would have a vision of a painting in my head when I awoke. The visionary painting would then just flow from my brushes onto the canvas almost effortlessly. Not having had much experience with artists, I thought all artists went through this physical and mental ritual. I never gave it a second thought or tried to analyze it. I just knew that getting my painting assignments done was easy if I went through this process. The instructor nearly always found the results favorable at the weekly critique.

Looking back to the writing assignments that I did in school, even as early as third or fourth grade, I remember getting my ideas during the middle of the night. I especially remember one story I wrote in the third or fourth grade because my peers criticized its length, but in the same breath told me how much they liked it. My assignment was to write a fictional story at least two pages long. My finished product was about fifteen pages in length. The feeling of the fun of writing that story is with me yet today. I had not given any thought to its length until the next day when the teacher told us that everyone was to read his or her story to the class. I was somewhat shy and very sensitive to criticism. As I read my story, I felt I was reading it for the first time. I attributed this confusion and loss of memory of its content to the fear of reading "my creation" in front of my peers. Now after many years and much study of the creative process, I realize it was not fear that caused the story to be new to me.

The same type of visions I had in my painting I experienced in my writing with the difference being my writing visions came into my mind in movie form. The paintings I saw were in the form of slides. I merely wrote the dialogue and described the scenery and characters of my mental movie. Not knowing any differently, I just assumed everyone had this experience. I still wonder if everyone does, but is just not aware of it.

Since this book contains poetry and rhymed messages, you may be interested in when the poetry or rhymed writing started. There was a time in high school English when we were studying poetry. During that period I got the urge to write my own poetry. These urges often came late at night or when I was sitting quietly outside in the sun.

One day while reading the "Ladies Home Journal" magazine, I saw an ad offering people the opportunity to submit a poem with the chance of it being published in the magazine. I believe there was a prize of $25, which to a teenager back then would have seemed like a lot of money. Not having a typewriter or knowing how to use one if I did, I hand wrote one of my poems and mailed it to the magazine. I told no one I had done this. In fact, you are the first people I have ever told. Several weeks later I received a short letter from the editor stating that at this time they could not use my poem. That letter ended my poetry writing for quite a number of years since criticism has always been a deadly poison arrow for me.

About five years ago I had an opportunity to go to Caymen Island for a two week stay at a friend's condominium. I had been receiving messages, consciously, from my spirit guides (or as many of you prefer to call them angels) for quite some time. Every morning I talked to my guides and wrote down their messages or guidance for me. One morning in Caymen as I was sitting on the balcony, listening to the surf, words started coming to me very rapidly. I asked that the guides slow down so I could write them more legibly. They patiently accommodated me.

The messages came in rhymed phrases, poems. I was having so much fun that my pen seemed to dance across the page to the cadence of the poem. Most of these poems were short and simple. I have included a few examples of these first rhymes in this book. I have, since, continued writing these rhymed messages nearly every morning.

Some of my current messages are telling me that I am now to share these rhymes with you. My third grade and "Ladies Home Journal" fears of criticism and rejection have been conquered. The importance of the messages via these poems far overrides my over sensitive ego's fears.

From the hundreds of rhymed messages, my spiritual board of directors and I have chosen a sampling from an enormous range of subject matter. The paintings and drawings scattered throughout the book were also co-created by my spiritual staff and me.

Enjoy, for these messages were sent to all of us with Love. You will recognize which one or ones are especially for you.

Claudette and "The Boys"

"The Boys" is a nickname Claudette affectionately calls her numerous spirit guides, although they are not of any gender.

Fly with Me

Even before my trip to the Caymen Islands, which is where the rhymed messages first appeared, I had been receiving, intuitively, the phrase, "Come fly with me". At the time I was not certain if this was an airline jingle I was remembering or if this message had a more prolific meaning.

As I discovered later, it was a prolific wake up call. I have included some of those early simplistic rhymed wake up calls as well as some of the messages that came later.

Not everyone needs to travel to the Caymen Islands to be awakened. Maybe, because there were no outside interference's such as phone calls or unexpected visitors, the Caymen retreat helped me to become a more open receiver.

First Rhymed Writing at Caymen

As I always do when I receive messages, I ask to whom am I talking. I was especially curious because of the rhymed format.

Caymen, Who is this?

This is a friend from above
I am here to bring you love
A smile is a gift
It eases the rift
Come fly with us
It is better than the bus
Your worry will leave
As you believe
This is fun
For we have begun

Rhymed Message

When you know that you are rare
You will not even have a care
For in time you will know
To listen to the crow
He sits atop a pole
And takes on his natural role
Because his eyes are cross
He often is the boss
He sees both sides the same
And therefore sees no shame
So when you hear him speak
Remember he, too, is the meek

The poetic messages, "The Call" and "Fly" came after I was home. Early one morning, (my spirit guides do not realize I am not a morning person) I was awakened by the loudest honking of geese I have ever heard. An alarm clock would appear silent compared to the noise those birds were making. Intuitively, I was prompted to pick up my pen and paper. That gaggle of geese honked the entire time I was writing "The Call". When I finished, there was silence. Talk about a wake up call.

The message "To Fly" comes occasionally even today. Since receiving it the first time, I have physically and spiritually flown., physically all over the world; spiritually to heights and depths I never could have imagined. Either way, my spiritual guides always fly beside me.

The Call

*A gaggle of geese
Through the window sends their sound.
They call, "Fly with us now,
In one place you are not bound,"*

*But in what direction should I fly
I'd like to know.
Should I fly high
Or should I fly low?*

*Again and again
They beckon to me,
Urging me to release my confines
And fly toward the sea,*

*What kind of power keeps me
Bound in place
When I can see breaking it
Would give me the freedom of space.*

*What is this I feel coming
Through my skin?
Oh yes, I see it is a tiny wing
That is very thin.*

Now another breaks through
And they start to flutter,
Stronger and stronger they get
As my cage starts to moan and mutter.

The cage is now starting to disappear,
Soon I'll take off into the sky,
No longer must I know
Where or why,

The ethers lift me
As higher and higher I sail,
No longer do I fear
That I will fail,

No longer do I worry
Which way to the sea,
For all the answers
Are there, now that I am free

Fly

*Fly little bird,
High, let yourself fly.
Spread your wings
And soar through the sky.*

*Feel the start
Of a whole new day.
No longer grounded,
You are on your way.*

*From above
You can "see" forever.
Any storm,
You now can weather.*

*No longer does the nest
Hold you with fear.
From the binds that hold you,
You now can sear.*

*The sun glistens
On the tips of your wings.
It penetrates as sweet notes
From your soul sings.*

Must you land?
You ask the sun.
Being aloft
Is so much fun.

The glow you have,
To the earth, must be brought,
For those with no wings
find that darkness is fought.

Without your songs
Those on earth would be deaf.
Silence would reign
No hope would be lef'.

Lay your eggs
To hatch here on earth,
For the new life they bring
Is the true meaning of birth.

So fly little bird.
Fly ever so high,
But do not forget that without you
Many souls would die.

I Fired Doubting Thomas

The following poetic messages came when my negative ego was strong and in control. As most artists and writers have complained, sometimes I am overwhelmed with a wave of self doubt. This self doubt has also been called the creative block.

It was during one of these "Doubting Thomas" days when these poetic messages were written. The message I received was that the more I created, the more Universal energy (God energy) I allowed through me. The more Universal energy that came through me the stronger my higher self (God self) became.

Not everyone needs to express their higher self through painting or writing, but everyone does need to express their higher self. If it is suppressed that person could experience depression or blockage.

Now when self doubts arise, I immediately put "Doubting Thomas" on unemployment.

The Poet

*Words of beauty that flow from his pen
Is God's way of bringing love to men*

*Listen to the Poet he has a message to tell
His words for the soul do ring a bell*

*His words are but a song of love
Inspired, it's certain from above*

*His words pierce our heart with a gentle beat
And strips away the shaft from the wheat*

*Feel their spirit as they dance through your head
Feel their power as down a new path you are led*

*His message will, vague, only seem
If the radiance of their meaning you do not gleam*

*Read with your heart and give the mind a rest
Then the meaning of life won't be such a test*

*Thank the Poet for coming your way
For his words of Grace will Lighten your day*

The Artist

*The artist uses the spirit's eyes when she does see
She paints the true soul of the tree*

*The rhythm and arrangement of her strokes
Brings order to what, to most, seems broke*

*In another dimension she often does reside
She shows us what in nature is inside*

*As she splashes the color upon the page
She takes on the vibration of the sage*

*With the freedom of the wind she draws a line
Often denoting a feeling, as a sign of divine*

*She shows how in harmony are all nature's parts
The song that she paints plucks the strings of our hearts*

*The resonance of color makes each of us feel whole
The repetition of shapes guides us to our soul*

*Without the artist how empty our life would surly be
Without the artist the soul of God we may never see*

*Sometimes her creation brings to our eyes, a tear
For it helps us remember a time when we had no fear*

*She helps us to see through a colorful ray
That in God's light we can always stay*

Nature Beings

There is something very special about awakening before dawn, going outside and hearing the quiet. Then as the sky turns from black to gray and the final star fades, I hear the bird's first trill. Long before the sun shows itself, I actually hear each petal, each blade of grass and each leaf stretch and awake.

I remember even as a child, sneaking outside in the wee hours of the morning, walking through the dew covered grass, sitting in it and talking to the flowers as they turned their faces toward the rising sun.

Even now I find I can get many of my questions answered, if I take the time to talk and listen to nature. For me, nature is especially verbal at dawn. Or could it be that at that time I am just more open to listening?

The following poems are a few of the communications I have had with various nature beings on this earth.

The Teachers

*Like a colorful quilt
The leaves cover the ground
But soon the North Winds
Do blow them to a mound*

*The trees are stripped
Of their camouflage
Their souls are exposed
Like an Earthly mirage*

*Like sentries they stand
The brunt of the Wind
Bending and swaying
Abuse they do fend*

*They know they are secure
As the Earth clings to their roots
Any pain or stress
Is soothed by her flutes*

They know if they withstand
There is a season of Hope
With perseverance and patience
They learn to cope

Ever reaching, they break
Through the mist
And let the gold of the sun
The darkness to resist.

The gold warmth moves
Through their trunks to the Earth
Their soul then celebrates
Another rebirth.

Like the trees
Let us learn to stretch and reach
Let the gold, our souls, penetrate
As thus they do teach

Story of a Tree

Life is very much like a tree
One is even like the life of thee

Toward the sky it reaches up high
Often it catches what does there fly

When its roots are buried deep in the earth
It stands strong and sturdy from its birth

When the roots are shallow it could easily fall
It is only then, it does not grow tall

Many a limb does grow from its trunk
On them the birds do find a bunk

With gratitude, they sing the tree a song
They grow together and do not think it wrong

Even the wind can not blow them over
When their roots are deep under the clover

Sometimes a limb is to them of no need
They simply grow another with which to feed

Sometimes its trunk becomes scarred with age
It only means it has the status of a sage

Its leaves or needles do catch the sun
Along the limbs they often do run

The sun warms it to its core
Where the tree spirit lives is the lore

Sometimes it is cut down to the ground
But by then it has scattered its seeds all around

Its spirit lives on in another form
It never dies; no need for alarm

With love we send this story of a tree
For you see, it could also be thee

This message was received while I was in the small mountain town of Hanmer, New Zealand. Very large, old and stately trees lined the streets.

Orchid Show

*Violets, pinks, yellows and the purist white
When orchids show their color, it is quite a sight*

*Their sweet alluring scent beckons you to approach
A captive of their magic as their energy you encroach*

*Some seem to point with a lip that hangs low
Some seem to laugh from their heart that is a glow*

*Truly a fashion show for all who gaze
A stripe, a dot, an occasional two tone causes one to daze*

*Some stand proud and erect, still others bend to please
Some lure you much closer as much would a tease*

*A group of tiny ones gather to cover a limb
While some grow to be wide, others prefer slim*

*Some hide their heart for few to see
Others declare to the world; my heart is open to thee*

*A few adorn themselves with ruffles and lace
Others prefer to more emphasize their face*

*Even within a family, never is one the same
For being different, there is never a blame*

*They give each other as much space as they need
For they realize they all came from the same seed*

*Oh, how glorious I would be, to be an orchid with but one goal
That, of only bringing pleasure to many, as I touch their soul*

*This message was received from the orchids at the annual orchid show
at the St. Louis Botanical Gardens.*

Forces of Nature

The forces of nature have always been a mystery to man. Our insurance policies even refer to them as "acts of God". I often wonder what is not an "act of God."

Science explains the more dramatic "acts of God" as fronts, throughs, El Ninos, inversions and so on. I prefer to see them as a mirror of my soul or inner being. When it rains, I feel it must be time to do a little emotional cleansing. When the sun is shinning bright, I feel I need to bring in more of the Golden Light. When it snows, maybe it is time to look at my uniqueness. A tornado prompts me to whirl away the negativity around me. When I witness a dawn, it tells me I am about to experience a new beginning.

Thunder helps all the energy vortexes in my body to open and resonate together. By the way, thunder is not a bowling alley for angels as my grandmother told me when I was a child. However, I still want to believe that there really is a pot of gold at the end of the rainbow.

I look at these forces of nature as a positive medicine for the mending of my soul. Without these demonstrative "acts of God", my soul's care and upkeep would be much more difficult.

Dawn

There is death like stillness just before dawn's light appears
The quiet is deafening as nature prepares to change gears

If one listens closely, he can hear her start to stretch
As she raises her head, the sun's rays to catch

Although snug and warm under her blanket of snow
She peeks her head through, to witness God's light show

With each ray of gold she becomes more alive
For nothing remains dead when dawn does arrive

Anticipation

The quiet of the darkness
Fills my room
In anticipation as on the brink
Dawn does loom.

My heart beats faster
With the first sign of light.
Shadows start to fade
As it grows ever bright.

Through my windows
The golden rays stream
And lifts my soul
With its soothing beam

All my concerns start
To melt away
For with every dawn
I start a new day

Morning Rain

*The quiet that comes
After a morning rain
Helps me to realize life
Need not be full of pain.*

*Only then do I hear
The peace within.
To everything, do I now
Feel a kin.*

*A small part of the whole,
I, but feel now
Humility reigns,
As I hand God a towel.*

*The rivers are full
In which I can flow.
The debris is cleared
So now I do know.*

*A morning rain,
What a beautiful event.
I thank you God.
I see now your true intent.*

Musical Show

Do you hear the music that comes from the hills
Or are you more concerned with paying the bills

Is not life but a musical show
The music starts playing and the actors glow

A beautiful harmony is the result
If another's rhythm they do not insult

This is God's song, he sets the key
To be in harmony make it the same for thee

Ping on the Pane

Listen closely to the raindrops ping on the pane
As the universe sheds a tear to lesson the strain

The woes of the world it washes away
In puddles like mirrors it shows you the way

Each drop, a different tone to the ear
For it carries within it, your joy or your fear

They harmonize together for this is your life
They blow together like husband and wife.

As the sun then replaces these tears from the sky .
You will see the golden reflection of your God tie.

Oh Sun

Oh Sun, Oh Sun,
Oh my dearest Sun!
You, who does bring life
To everyone.

Your warm rays shine
Deep into my soul.
You light the task
Of my earthly goal.

Even when I am
In the shadow of a cloud,
Your Love shines through
Your voice is loud.

Is your light eternal
Or should I fear the Dark?
Though my soul seems to remember
Your eternal spark.

Your rays lift the mist
That veils my Love.
Glory and Peace reign in my life
When you are above.

Cold Snowy Morn

*As one looks out on a cold snowy morn
All is quiet as though nothing is born*

*Then through the golden ray, God casts His Love down
And everything on Earth wears a golden crown*

*A crown so lovely it is studded with jewels
The colors they bear follows God's natural rules*

*All is cloaked with lace of silver and gold
For this is divine clothing, we are told*

*Piercing the silence the caw of a crow, the coo of a dove
Announces to the world wake up and feel the love*

*As we awake from what seems as eternal sleep
We recognize life's joy and into action we leap*

*O h, how glorious it is to be again born
And to see only life's wonders and not its scorn*

*As a peacock, wear your golden crown with pride
And in God's chariot take a joyous ride.*

The Crow

For quite a while, I have been aware of my special relationship with the crows and the ravens. They have guided me in the spiritual as well as the physical world.

Sometimes when I am driving around searching for a certain address, the largest crow I have ever seen will be standing on the side of the road. As I pass him, he will fly in the direction I need to travel so as to arrive at my desired destination. Then, if I need to turn, he will fly in circles at the intersection of my turn.

Those of you who still believe in coincidences may think that is all I am experiencing. Maybe, if this had only happened once or twice, I might think so myself. But these sleek black magical birds of prey have shown me the way again and again.

The crow has also shown me the way spiritually. Often during meditation, he will fly into my mind's eye and help me to go to a deep level where everything is blissful and clear. Sometimes when I wander off my true path he will sound his shrill caw and flap his noisy wings over my head. When this happens, I do stop and change gears and listen to my higher self for a new direction. The crow's caw is not exactly subtle or easy to ignore.

When the poem "Caw" was written, I was walking in a park. I heard the cawing of the crow over head. Actually, who wouldn't. As I came to a bench, a feather floated down not more than six inches from my nose. It hesitated there long enough for me to pick it out of the air. I sat on the bench and words to the poem "Caw" floated onto the paper. As I finished the last line, my crow friend who was minus one feather circled over my head as if to say.

"Good job, you got the message."

I am extremely grateful, for no matter where I am in the world, the crow or his brother the raven are there to guide me to that empty place within, where we find what we often call the void. Helping me find directions on the road is just an added bonus. I know that, if the crow is near, true magic of all kinds is about to happen.

Signals

*The caw of the crow signals an alert within
Be aware my dear, your protection is thin*

*A helping hand is fine and good
But for barracudas it could be food*

*Take a look and see what is truly real
It is a time of discerning or you could be the meal*

*No harm will come, if you heed the caw (call)
You may stumble a bit, but we will catch your fall*

Caw (Call)

*In the Void you will see
How everything, eventually, comes "to be"*

*Enjoy the moment and live for today
It eliminates the worry of going the "wrong" way*

*The woes of the past serve no purpose right now
It merely causes a wrinkle on the brow*

*It makes no difference in what location you live
No matter where you are, if centered, the universe will give*

*Create the environment in which you feel joy
For the game of life is merely a toy*

*Pleasing others feeds the ego, it is true
However, without the approval, the ego is blue*

*Judging the path that others should take
Is like giving someone a loaded cake*

*The Crow gives a call (caw) to come to alert
So the spirit will awaken and not be inert*

*He says to follow him where you can create
So take his lead and in life's joy take a stake*

*Going to the Void causes the ego to fear
For it looses its power in there, my dear*

The bliss that you seek is there, if you believe
So take that step and be ready to receive

Like the magician the crow is cloaked in black
A spiritual color if, in history, you will look back

Drink in the wisdom of this black winged friend
For a messenger of God is his true intend

When his magic is used for a higher good
The Light gets very bright around your hood

In a never ending circle the Crow often does fly
Showing you thus, that eternal life is not a lie

So next time you hear that familiar caw (call)
Listen carefully to the message because, One, we are all

With love we send the wise Crow's tale
For he keeps on cawing(calling) even when you do "fail"

A Message from the Crow

What is your message, my friend the Crow
You have beckoned me with you caw, now yourself do show

I hear your silence, it's deafening to my ear
I come in peace, from me you have nothing to fear

Did you bring me here to show me the buds of Spring
Or to show me what joy, a daffodil can bring

I watch you as you strut with a mate
Always there to protect her from an ill fate

Perched high on a branch you watch with eyes that cross
As she builds her nest with twigs and bits of moss

Share you magic I am here to receive
Show me how I, in my own magic, can believe

The shrill of your caw beckons me to you side
Tell me your secrets, to your words I will abide

To the void show me the way
For it is only there that I can create today

I watch as you soar and circle above
Are you showing me? Life never ends when it's created with love

A few words from Claudette:
On the morning this was written I was awakened by the sharp shrill "Caw" of a Crow outside my bedroom window. As I sipped on a cup of coffee, the above words flowed from my pen. I felt as though I was engulfed in a cocoon of warm loving liquid energy which penetrated every cell of my body and soul.
Although this is a message for me, I feel by sharing it, some of you will receive the same sense of Hope and Joy that I experienced.
Listen for your "Caw" (Call).

What's a Crystal?

Sometime ago, at a meeting I was attending, someone handed me a small crystal and said, " I think you need this." I took it, thinking what am I to do with it and why do I need it? It did not seem like the proper time or place to reveal my ignorance by asking these questions.

Later while browsing through a bookstore, I came across a book on crystals and bought it. Reading the book, I discovered that crystals actually come out of the ground with points and facets. I feel sure enough of myself now to admit that I thought then they were all cut by man and used primarily for lamps and vases.

That little crystal gift was the beginning of an insatiable quest for greater knowledge and understanding of this brilliant little piece of nature.

In a meditation group, I witnessed several people holding a crystal in their hand while they meditated. After meditation a few of the people told the group that they had received information through the window in the crystal. Others said their crystal was talking to them, giving them messages. Then others made comments like, "It's an Isis crystal or a smoky quartz, or a twin or a deva, etc." At this, I knew it was time for another book.

I, then, started collecting and working with crystals. I soon learned they really do have powers. And yes, they really do talk to you. I also found that none of this was new. The ancients speak of these abilities in many of their legends. I was finding I was getting the most profound messages while holding various crystals in my hand. I was hooked. I started buying crystals of all shapes and sizes.

At another meeting someone was talking about their recent trip to Hot Springs, Arkansas, to dig crystals. They talked about digging in the mud and bringing home a basket full of these gems. She showed us one still covered with the red clay. I was amazed. I had no idea that just anyone could find and dig crystals out of mud. Didn't you need a degree in mining or something? This sounded like an adventure I wanted to experience.

One weekend two of us drove to Hot Springs to go digging. I now know what it must have felt like to the miners of the gold rush era. I became so excited by what the next shovel full of mud might contain that I forgot all about my basic bodily needs, like food and water. In my mind, I just knew that at any moment I was going to hit the motherload.

Since those first mining days, I have discovered that sitting on a mound of crystal filled red clay is one of the most therapeutic experiences I can have. The crystals I find is not as important as the inner peace and quiet that permeates through me as I am surrounded by all that glistening energy.

Over the years these faceted gems have truly become my friends. Now when I go on one of my therapeutic digs, certain of these friends will pop up and say "Take me home, I have something to tell you"

A Crystal

Beautiful crystal so bright and clear
Tell us your story we're ready to hear

Little one that tingles my hand
How long have you waited deep in the land

You give your energy so unconditionally and free
I am grateful you chose to work with me

Never dying and always alive
You teach me that the soul always does survive

Each one in your family is different from the rest
But I see now, there is never a best

You adore the sun and the moon too
You gather their energy and share it with not a few

Sometimes you hide a phantom inside
Or you might create a rainbow that is often wide

A few of you offer me a door to walk in
There, I do disscover there is no sin

You charge my batteries, you align the flow
After which, I feel the celestial glow

Oh, little mighty one I thank you for being my friend
You comfort me so, when my human life I do tend

As I hold and caress you, I start to zing
For in my heart your love does sing

After a while I know you must move on
But shortly there after, you send your son

With love I want you to know, I appreciate your gifts
They help to smooth the bumps and the rifts

The Butterfly

One balmy morning while visiting Lin, a friend in the Chicago area, I decided to treat myself to some time in the sun on her patio. As per usual I gathered my morning equipment, a cup of coffee and my pen and paper. I then situated myself comfortably in a lawn chair.

The peace and quiet, broken only by the rustle of her may trees and the early morning serenade of the birds, was the perfect therapy for what I knew would later be a rather demanding day.

It had been my ritual for years to write every morning any messages I might receive from my spirit guides. That particular morning nothing much was coming through to me. Then out of the corner of my eye, I spotted a large monarch butterfly. The intricate design on his wings intrigued me. All I could think was what a beautiful painting or piece of fabric the design would make.

As I sat there day dreaming, this glorious butterfly flew to my shoulder. I picked up my pen and the words to the poem, "The Mentor" flowed onto the paper. That distinguished monarch stayed on my shoulder until the last word was written. At that time it flew to a nearby flower and perched himself on a petal as though waiting. A smile came to my face as I thanked him and my "other" guides for the inspirational message. The butterfly fluttered his wings in response and flew away. As it shared this message with me, I in turn share it with you. May it warm your heart and bring a tear of hope to your eye as it did to me, for our messengers come in many forms.

My Mentor

*Fly little butterfly,
Flutter your wings.
Sweetest of nectars the flowers
To you brings*

*No longer a cocoon
Binds you in place.
The whole world can now
Be your space*

*You sparkle so,
With the rays of the sun.
Now your main purpose
Is to merely have fun.*

*You appear to be
So fragile and frail,
As from place to place
You do sail.*

*But you know what it is
To struggle and grow.
And then to break loose
Of the ties that bind you so.*

*What are the messages written
In the pattern on your wing?
Why when you're near,
Do we feel the newness of Spring?*

The Mentor

*Every moment you are free
You adventure forth without a care,
You say it is now time to enjoy,
   You have paid the fare.*

*You have no fear of the death
   That must take place;
   For now is the time
   And here is the space*

*What a mentor and comfort
   You have been to me,
Thank you for teaching me
   How to live free.*

Lake Titicaca

High in the Andes, about 12,000 feet, I put on my lama sweater, my wool poncho and topped myself with the lama fur hat I had bought out the window of our tour bus the day before. I was ready for the brisk four hour boat ride to the middle of Lake Titicaca. Even though the sun was shinning, the temperature was not much above freezing.

Along with my fellow travelers, I boarded one of the two small boats which was to take us to that special destination. Our crew, two small Peruvian Indians dressed in their native costumes, started the engine. With the chug chug of the motor and the nauseating smell of gasoline fumes, our adventure began. The view of the mountains surrounding the lake and an occasional passing reed boat kept us entertained.

After a while, the people on the boat started chatting. Someone mentioned that it would be exciting if we saw one of the often seen space craft going into the water. Evidently there are legends of an underwater city in the middle of this high mountain lake. The natives take as a matter of fact the coming and going of the water people in their space crafts. They consider them somewhat divine or deities much as the Greek, Romans and Biblical writers considered the beings who came to earth from the sky.

The boat chatter quieted down. I asked my friend, Bill, how would we know when we were over this legendary city under the water. His answer was to ask my spirit guides. So I did. After connecting with them, the guides told me that I would know we were over the city when the water turned warm and I heard music. This lake is a glacier fed lake. The water should never be warm. The music I had to hear to believe. Being a skeptic is a challenge for my spirit guides.

As we putt putted along, every so often, I would put my hand in the water being careful not to fall in. Another part of the legend is that if anyone falls in the lake, he is not to be retrieved because it meant that the water people wanted them. I did not want to test the legend.

After about four hours out, I put my hand in the water. It was warm. I could not believe it, so I told Bill to put his hand in also. It was warm. Then I heard music. Bill did not hear the music, but someone on the other boat yelled out that he was hearing music. They, also, exclaimed that the water was warm. With these confirmations, I decided to "ring up" the city below through telepathy, a gift I had only in the last few years consciously discovered that I had.

The voices came through loud and clear, almost as though I had an ATT phone implanted. When the water people first started talking, I felt a rush of extremely loving energy engulf me. I gave Bill a pen and paper and asked if he would write down my questions and their answers as I talked to my new acquaintances. The information came fast, but he was able to scribble down the essence of the two way conversation as I talked quietly outloud.

They were so interesting and loving, I could have talked to them forever. I was ready to let the water people take me, but they said I could not at this time visit because my three dimensional body would not survive the higher vibrations of their city. They did say at some time soon I would be ready, as would a great number of the earthlings. They said the changes in the vibration of the earth would help us to raise our vibrations.

I asked what I, as well as others, could do to raise our vibrations. There answer was to let go of my fears.Simple but not so easy.

I have included in this book a painting of these near light beings. Maybe, you, too, have met them or one of their earthling ambassadors. My Maori friends in New Zealand have known them for a long time, but the story of the six fingers and cobalt blue eyes will be told later.

Our Peruvian Boatmen

Highly Evolved Astronaut

Messengers

*Who are these foreigners in their spaceships
They have no mouths or even lips*

*Their eyes are bright, a radiant blue
Of what world are they a crew*

*A gentle lot, but so big and strong
They never tell me I am right or wrong*

*Why have they come here I constantly ask
Their only reply. "For a Divine task"*

*Why are we taught to fear these souls so kind
Is it just the unknown that warps our mind*

*They tell me they are here to help dispel fear
But only when we ask. They are not to interfere*

*They seem so familiar, have I know them before
I believe it was when to another dimension, I found a door*

Messengers

The ancients spoke of them coming on a large bird of white
All over the world they spoke of the same sight

Messenger, angels, some did call
From the sky they said they did fall

They are here again in a very large force
To help us to alter our destructive course

They help us to understand that there is hope
They help us to understand that with change we can cope

We thank these beings in their mystical white robes
Who come from afar in ships with light strobes

We ask them to help us hear their message of how to toss
This time we promise not to nail them to a cross

The Reed People
On Lake Titicaca

Unless you have actually walked on a reed island, it would be difficult to imagine how it would feel. It is constantly moving and rocking. To me it felt as though I was walking on foam rubber.

These mountain people of Peru live everyday on islands made of only matted reeds. They also make their boats from this same material that is so prevalent to the region. Their boats glide through the water staying perfectly dry inside. Even their houses are constructed from these limber but strong reeds. To think, we consider them to be weeds. While for these quiet, gentle people, they are primary to their existence.

Could the reed people be some of the survivors from a Lemurian outpost? Some of their spiritual beliefs are similar to those of the American Indian, the New Zealand Maori, the Tibetan Nomad and the Mexican Indian. Many of their weavings and carvings could have been found in these other lands. The symbols they use vary only slightly.

All of these people surrounding the Pacific Ocean seemed to have recognized, as familiar, the necklace I designed and had made. Some of the Peruvians wondered why I had turquoise stones in it since according to their beliefs only the elders of their tribes are allowed to wear turquoise. I was asked more than once during my stay in Peru if I would trade it.

All of these cultures speak openingly and matter of faculty of people from another planet. Another similarity I found fascinating is that they all revere a great white bird. Could they still be waiting for it to come? Maybe.

A reed island home on Lake Titicaca in Peru. Notice a misty looking shape near the back of the woman. I can only guess what it is. I do know that it was not smoke or mist.

Claudette dressed for the eight hour boat trip ride on Lake Titicaca

Machu Picchu , Peru

When I first heard about Machu Picchu I could not even pronounce the name. Certain people kept telling me I needed to go there. I did not know why I needed to go there, but it did sound like an adventure. Shortly after being told this, I received a brochure in the mail from a travel company advertising a tour to Peru, specifically Machu Picchu. Taking this as "too" coincidental, I signed up.

The following story was written on the plane coming home from my second trip to this land below the equator.

Machu Picchu
An Incan Holiday Inn

Machu Picchu, the ruins of an ancient civilization, is situated high in the Andes mountains overlooking the Urubamba River in Peru. After taking a train from Cusco to Agnes Clientes, our group boarded a bus which traveled up the face of a mountain decorated with wild orchids and small waterfalls. At the top were ruins of what must have been a fairly large city. If one were to listen to the Peruvian guides, one would be somewhat confused as to who really built and lived in this ancient mystical city in the sky. Most of the guides, depending on their heritage, credit the Incas for this miraculous architectural feat and blame the Spanish for destroying it.

When examining the structures, I found it obvious that there were at least three or four builders. The following information is what I channeled while sitting in one of the buildings whose granite stones are so precisely cut and fitted together that a thin piece of paper could not be inserted between them. Some of the stones are even polygonial.

(Channeled information) Machu Picchu was a civilization constructed by ancient astronauts from another planet. People from a dieing planet were deposited there. These ancient astronauts were from another galaxy beyond what we, as earthlings are able to conceive at this time. These distant astronauts of a higher demension have the ability to change matter. At Machu Picchu, they changed rocks into a more pliable form, then back into its original solid rock form. This explains the preciseness of the rock construction. This city was constructed as an outpost for Lemuria, which was the center for this highly evolved civilization.

The Lemurian outpost was given the same symbols and knowledge that these giant astronauts had. These evolved teachers from Lemuria taught the transplanted people about eternal life and about how everything and everyone is one with the creator. They taught that when all were working in balance with each other, there was no struggle or disease.

On the chests of these ancient teachers was the symbol of this unity. (This is the necklace, pictured under the story about New Zealand, that attracted the Maori woman..) The small circles were stones of turquoise reserved for the highest rank (spiritually evolved) "priests". Local priests were required to learn stringent lessons and initiations (tests) to earn the "right" to wear the turquoise stone. For each level of initiation, a different colored stone of a different vibration was used in the symbol.

Some outpost priests were transported to the Motherland, Mu or Lemuria, for intense testing and instruction before raising to another level of evolement. Machu Picchu was often visited by birds with large wings. Sometimes balls of red, blue, green or gold light was seen descending to the ground from these birds.

Comment from Claudette: These large winged birds still hover over this sight as I witnessed in my March 21, 1996 night visit to the ruins. Colored lights came and went, each time bringing an energy to the area that made my skin tingle. Even though it was quite chilly that night on this mountain top, I felt warm and content wrapped in a blanket of love like nothing I had ever felt before. The two other people sitting near me felt the same sennsation.

Channeled information continues: This loving existance as an outpost of Lemuria continued for thousands of years. Then one day the earth rumbled and the air filled with red rocks and gray smoke. Many people were sweep away and drowned in the swollen rivers. Many were killed by the falling rocks caused by the violent shaking of the earth. Some people of Machu Picchu survived the catastropic events. Some escaped to other areas while some found refuge in caves. They continued to look toward the sky for rescue. For years they lighted large fires as signals for the large birds so their whereabouts would be discovered. No one came from the sky to rescue them.

.After the earth stopped shaking and the water receded, these blond , once peaceful inhabitants of Machu Picchu, were found by a dark rather fierce group of people. They coerced these fair, loving refugees into directing them to the mountain top city or what was left of it. There they used the refugees as slaves to rebuild. Without the help of the "gods" from the "birds", the rebuilding was of a much cruder nature. When things did not proceed to their liking these new inhabitants of Machu Picchu used sacrificial rituals in order to please the angry "gods".

What was once a peaceful, balanced, loving and quite spiritually evolved culture was now controled by a greedy and power oriented group of people who taught the original inhabitants to live in fear instead of love. This type of existance lasted through the generations until they were eventually conquered by the Incas after another similar earthly catastrophe. Machu Picchu was rebuilt again by the Incas and used primarily for a "Holiday Inn" by their heirarchy. Some of the Incan symbols and legends still denote references to the philosphy of those original people. These legends and symbols were known by the Incan priests. For control reasons, the common people were not allowed to either use the symbols or repeat the legends. (This rule still exists today in the tribes of many of the Peruvian mountain people.)

Later the Spanish conquered the Incas and plundered what was left of their symbolic artifacts, by now in the possession of the Incan priests.

Comments from Claudette: Even today, some of the Peruvian mountain people are waiting for the large white "bird" to come from the sky. They revere the Condor when it appears as a sacred symbol.

Machu Picchu has gone through many transitions, but the peceptive visitor to the ruins can still feel the love and peace of its original inhabitants. While sitting on the massive stones, many visitors receive a mental rememberance of when they, themselves were a part of the Lemurian spirit.

I have included a picture of Machu Picchu as well as one of its present day inhabitants who challenged me and won for space on a rock.

Sedona

The first time I saw Sedona, Arizona, was long before I knew what an energy vortex was. I was focusing my own energies on my painting, specifically watercolor. I had been teaching quite a few watercolor classes and I felt I needed to get away where I could completely focus on my own art. A watercolor workshop in Sedona, given by Zolton Szabo, offered me this opportunity.

An art friend and her husband and my husband and I flew to Phoenix from Denver, rented a car and drove to Sedona. It was dark when we arrived so it was not until the next morning that we saw the awesome buttes glimmering with hues of crimson and gold. Even meeting Jane Russell the night before took second billing to the grander of the scenery.

Every morning after breakfast we began our art class and the husbands went golfing. Zolton sent us outside for an hour to gather subject matter. Then we were to come back to the class and paint for the remainder of the day under his instruction. Some days I became so absorbed in the gathering that I did not return for two or three hours. Needless to say this action did not make me the teacher's pet. While in the canyons, time stood still, at least my time.

By the end of the week I had personally connected with the souls of most of the buttes surrounding Sedona and a lot of the trees and rocks in Oak Creek Canyon. The connection with Oak Creek, itself, was so close, it felt as though the river flowed through my veins instead of blood.

That trip to Sedona was so inspiring that I painted its landscape for years. Whenever my creative ideas would wane, I found myself painting a butte or a part of Oak Creek. I may had come home to Denver physically, but part of my soul still remained in Sedona.

Several years later, after I knew what a vortex was, I physically returned to Sedona with a friend. It felt like I was returning home. At the time my, life was in a transition; new job, new marriage status and a new living location. There was so much new, I was not sure I knew who I was any more.

When we arrived in Sedona, I called a new friend I had met in St. Louis, who had recently moved there. He introduced me to my first vortex experience. As every good tour guide does in Sedona, he took us to the top of the airport vortex and then down to the other side. On paper this sounds easy, but if you have a fear of heights and live near sea level, this is a major emotional and physical accomplishment. Gathering all the will power I could, I followed him out onto the overhang where he felt we needed to be to meditate. It was a place most tourist never visited because of the steepness of the rocks.

All of us found "our" spot along the edge of the cliff. A couple of deep breaths and closing my eyes relaxed me enough to go into a meditative state. I asked for guidance in over coming my fear of heights, mainly because I knew at some point I would get hungry, the sun would set, my meditation would end and I would have to get back down off the mountain.

The guidance came. As I drifted into a altered state, I saw, in my mind's eye, myself falling off the cliff head over heels all the way to the bottom. As I saw myself die, instead of feeling fearful, I felt peaceful. Dying was all right, almost joyful. This peacefulness stayed with me even after I came out of meditation.

I was sitting there in my blissfulness when my eyes were drawn to the ground on my left. There sat the brightest turquoise lizard I have ever seen. Actually, it was the only turquoise colored lizard I had ever seen. At the time, I thought it was my imagination, but now I know better. That little lizard which sat about four inches from me was congratulating me for conquering the biggest fear anyone can have (maybe the only fear), the fear of death. From that moment on, I have been on one adventure after another. That little lizard has been with me no matter where I go in the world, reminding me that when I gave up the fear of death, I also gave up my fear of life.

I think everyone has a special place or places they go where magical things take place. Find your place whether it is Sedona, Machu Picchu, Tibet or Podunkville, USA. Anywhere or everywhere could be your power place where your magic happens.

A Mystic Place

*Red Rocks surrounded a valley
That did shimmer.
The gifts that were given
Were abundant with glimmer,*

*You gazed at the stars
And traveled the skies.
When you spotted the blue one
There was quite a sigh,*

*The magical waters of Oak Creek
Helped you to heal throughout.
That is what
An adventure is all about,*

*Your human guide knew the ways
Of the ancient ones.
Soon he will be reaching
Beyond the suns.*

*Digest all
That you've seen, heard and felt,
And soon all your human worries
Will start to melt,*

*A vortex you felt
It was quite a jolt
Your vibrations are raising,
Do not revolt.*

*Spread the wisdom
And the energy you brought back,
It is of little use
If it's kept in a sack,*

A Mystic Place

Retouch with this mystical area
When you start to sag,
Gather the energy
And refill your bag,

Look about from that higher step
On which you now stand,
Touch the crystals
Within the sand,

Blow to the North,
South, East, and West,
Bring in the Spirit,
It knows what is best,

Ride the waves
And with the spirit do flow,
Enjoy every moment
And take it slow,

The symbols you saw
Do tell a story,
It was a time
Of bliss and glory,

Some symbols are missing
So travel back to that time,
You will see them
That most of us did talk in rhyme,

Do not compare
What the others did receive,
Your higher self knows
What you need to believe,

The Ravens brought magic
They were there to teach,
They soared quite low
So you could reach,

A Mystic Place

Until your next journey
We bid you farewell,
Let the Cliff Rose be
Your connecting smell.

Pictographs in Sedona

Stratas of Red

Stratas of red pierce a sky so blue
Buttes that resemble an object or two

Hawks circle lazily looking for prey
In the valley their victims unaware lay

The smell of pine permeates the air
Sending us its fragrance as at the scenery we stare

What history the rocks and the trees do hold
What stories in the wall paintings are told

Pockets of energy burst from the land
At vortexes eager searchers band

Ruins of ancients stand crumbled in the cliffs
By gone peoples who could not settle there riffs

Are they sending a message as we examine the past
Was it not greed and control the reason they did not last

Entering the door to a better place
Is one way to see there can be a more peaceful place

Feeling compassion for all on this earth
The only way to assure having within, true love to birth

The Wizard

I have always been fascinated with the story of Merlin, the wizard who seemed to have lived forever. Since most legends are more truth than fiction, I started looking into just who this Merlin was and just what were his talents.

Through my travels and reading, I have discovered that most ancient, as well as some modern, cultures have their own version of a Merlin. The Native Americans as well as other Central and South American Cultures have their medicine men or women or shaman. Still, other cultures may call these wizards, witch doctors, gurus, lamas, priests, faith healers chieftains, messiahs, yogis or whatever title the culture decides to label this member of their tribe or group.

The name may be different but all the wizards have specially developed talents. Most all of them are seers. They see and predict the future. Although often using different tools and rituals such as "magic" potions, they are all healers. They create "miracles".

A great amount of power was given to these ancient wizards, not too different from the power we often give our doctors and clergymen in our modern times.

Through the various classes and books I have studied, I have discovered that I, too, have the abilities to create "miracles" and do "magic". Through the teaching I have done, I have discovered that everyone without exception on this planet and maybe other planets, has the ability to heal, do "magic", see the future and to do whatever the ancient wizards were said to have been able to do.

A whole new world opened up for me when I awakened my wizard within. My life became full of hope and joy. This awakening within me is what inspired the poem, "The Wizard".

Wizard

Where is that wizard of which many speak
Will he show himself or is he a sneak

I want to see some of his magic tricks
I want a miracle that to my soul, it sticks

Where does he live, does he have a home
Or through the forest does he just roam

Why can't I see him, am I really that blind
If so, please help to open my eyes and mind

Let him come forward and face me eye to eye
Then I won't doubt or think him a lie

Oh! There he is, I feel him close by
Will he always respond to my pleading cry

Could it be that he hides deep within me
And only comes forth, when I'm willing to see

I feel his love as his wand passes over my heart
He knew just what I needed, he is so smart

Thank you dear wizard, my loving friend
Thank you for helping, my life to contend

Transformation

Most of us allow our family or society to mask and mold us into something we truly are not? I know I did. However, many times I have found the courage to remove the mask and reveal who I truly am. Not once have I regretted it.

The poem "Make Believe" tells of one such transformation that I experienced. This message helped me to realize more fully that we are never too old or is it too late to transform and let the inner child be born again.

Make Believe

Who am I?
And what will I be
Asks every child
By the time they are three,

We give them costumes
To play make believe,
If they wear them long enough
They, then, will receive,

We give them a mask
To hide who they are
Then say take it off
And you won't go far,

The longer they wear it;
The longer they do mold
Until without it they are nothing
They are told,

Some find the courage
To take the mask off,
But then often family and friends
Do thus scoff

Alone in the world
They start building new dreams.
With this new identity
Their ego shrills these screams,

"How dare he change
After all these years.
I'm accustomed to operating
With the feeling of fears,"

But on deaf ears
These screams do fall,
For this child's self-confidence
Is no longer small,

Without the mask
This child starts to clearly see,
That it is only "he"
Who he wants "To Be",

So Familiar

Often in our lives we meet people who seem familiar. We search our memory for a key to where we have met them before. Sometimes we even "accidentally" refer to them by a different name excusing the mistake with some comment like, "I'm not very good with remembering names",

I have had many of these experiences with various people. While talking to a friend one day, I suddenly saw him in a different body in another time. The mental movie lasted for several minutes.

Prior to my mental movie starting, I had been irritated with something he had said. Until that lapse into what many call a past life regression where he and I had experienced a similar scenario to the present one, I did not fully understand why I felt so irritated with him. Once I saw I was repeating the same reaction as I had in that other life, I was able to change it. Doing so turned out to be for the betterment of all. By the way, that particular past life scenario ended tragically for everyone especially me.

I had read the Eastern philosophy of karmic return, but had never really understood the full impact of it on our daily lives until that and other very graphic personal experiences. I thank the universe for lifting my veil of amnesia. Without the revealment of that past life, my intense irritation with that man may have resulted in the termination of what today is a close and loving relationship. By forgiving what happened in the past (myself as well as him), I am able to proceed with my life without the heavy burdens of that past emotional tramma.

The following poetic message came after one of these past life experience.

Together Again

You are so familiar, I know I knew you before,
Your body is different, but I recognize your core.

Tell me, why are we together again once more?
Is it merely to love or to settle a score?

Do try to remember, it will help me to see
Why I often feel you are so much a part of me,

I feel your pain and I feel your joy.
Were you back then, a girl or boy?

Your eyes are the same, I feel their glow,
And to my heart they strike a blow,

Why are the details so hard to remember,
If on the same team, we were often a member?

Your touch is familiar, I do remember it.
Wait! I think I'm remembering bit by bit,

Your were always there when I needed you most,
Of the sacrifices for me, you would never boast.

Thank you for being again by my side,
Thank you for showing me, eternal Love does abide,

A New Start

*All these words
Put on paper with pen
Help me to understand who I am
And where I have been,*

*I was a poet
And also a priest,
Sometimes on the spiritual scale
I was the least,*

*I put all together
These lessons I have learned,
Any past injustices
I have now burned,*

*On a fresh new start
I am about to embark,
The knowledge of the past
Will be my sprark*

*Without the regrets
To dampen my flame,
My fire will burn bright
For I have no one to blame,*

Who is Cassandra?

During many of my earlier meditations, I had heard the name, Cassandra. I would ask my guides, "Cassandra who?" or "What about Cassandra?" I received no answer. This dialogue was repeated many times throughout the years. Out of frustration and curiosity, I asked some of my intuitive friends why I kept hearing the name Cassandra. Without exception they came up blank.

One day while in the Cayman Islands, during a meditation, I again asked my guides, "Why am I always hearing the name, Cassandra?" The following rhymed message was given to me. When the last line was written I burst into tears. Something in the message struck me at a deep level, but I was still not quite sure why.

Cassandra in Caymen

(I asked who was Cassandra, a name I had gotten repeatedly during meditation. This was the answer from my guides)

*Cassandra is your name
And also your claim to fame*

*She came from a far away place
To join in the human race*

*A teacher to be
She started her lessons on Cree*

Cassandra

The epitome of kind
She had quite a mind

Some thought her a goddess
Others looked at her bodess

Remember, too, my dear
That you are now here

As you tell your story
You will dispense the worry

We love you now the same
As we did in your other frame

When I returned home, I asked a few people if they knew a woman named Cassandra from ancient history. Several mentioned that there was one during the Greek and Trojan sagas written by Homer. That was all I needed to stimulate my investigation quest.

I discovered that Cassandra is known in history for speaking the words "Beware of Greeks bearing gifts" (a phrase I have used many times not really knowing where it originated). These words she gave to their father, the king of Troy, when he asked her advice on whether to accept the Greek gift of the Trojan horse. Obviously, her father did not pay heed to her warning and the result was the downfall of Troy.

Cassandra was given the gift of prophecy by Apollo in exchange for her becoming his mistress. When she reneged on the agreement, he licked her lips so, although she had the gift of prophecy, no one would believe the words that came across her lips.

Since obtaining this historical and personal information, I am able to more readily trust, as accurate, the prophecies I receive and give. I am also able to receive gifts more unconditionally. I will admit, however, that I am still searching for Apollo. Any man who licks my lips or ever has is a primary suspect, although I do not know what I would say or do if I found him.

Becoming A Member of the Cast

From my sleeper sofa in the living room of the rented condominium in Hot Springs, Arkansas, I had a clear view through the sliding glass doors of Lake Hamilton. On this particular morning I awoke about six am. As I looked outside I saw a mist slowly moving over the land and the lake. It crawled along the surface of the land weaving through the trees. On the lake it rolled over the surface with only an occasional hole in its mass, so as to remind me that a body of water with a shore existed beneath it white fleece.

I was pulled by its mystic to the verandah. I let myself be enveloped by its gentleness. I let its arms wrap around me as it had done everything else in its path. It made me feel like a child wrapped in a blanket snuggled against her mother's breast. The longer I sat there, the more inner peace I experienced.

As the sun's rays pierced holes through this peaceful blanket, I received the words for the poem, "The Mist". The birds orchestrated the background music as the words danced onto the paper. The beams of the sun continued to spotlight the stage for this dramatic play of nature directed by who else but God.

The Mist

Mist that envelopes like a blanket of fleece
To our soul it brings calm and a feeling of peace.

So secure I feel as it softens the sharpness of the land,
Hidden behind its veil, time but a grain of sand.

From its pillow the sun starts to stretch its rays,
Piercing the veil, bringing golden light to the day.

Like a ray of love, it warms my chest,
Radiating through me, it spreads to the rest.

Songs of praise fill the air as this new day does awake.
Breezes of joy create ripples on the misty lake.

How small I feel as I resonate to the whole
And yet a significant part plays my little soul.

Who is the director of this award winning play?
Grant him his glory or behind the scene must he stay?

His direction is clear for those willing to hear.
His voice is soft, words never spoken with a blare.

To his stars he gives a crown of gold,
No bit players are in the stories through Him told.

Raise you curtain of mist and wear your crown,
Being a star in His play will create a smile not a frown.

The New Zealand Maori

If you have never seen the Maori of New Zealand perform their native songs and dances, it should be on your list of things to do in this lifetime. My friend, Bill and I arrived in Rotorua, a city on the west side of the north island of New Zealand, at about four p.m.. It is known for its hot, healing mineral baths, as well as its abundance of Moari culture.

I had visited this city about fifteen years earlier and had see a performance of Maori singers and dancers. I was so impressed then, that I wanted to repeat the experience. When we checked into the motel, the desk clerk offered to make the reservations for what the Maori call a Hangi Hahari. This is a feast along with ceremonial singing and dancing held in their ceremonial house. It can be a very emotional and moving event as well as a lot of fun.

The desk clerk with her proper Queen's English accent asked me to give her three choices from the twenty or more performances being held that evening. I gave her three. Trying to be helpful, she vetoed my first choice telling me it was too far out of town, since it was actually located on Maori land. Most of the performances are held at the large hotels in town. Ten minutes later she called our room to tell us she had tried all of the places and the only one that had an opening was my first choice. Imagine that. Maybe it was at that moment that I knew we were about to experience a very special night

The mini bus for the performance was to pick us up at six-thirty p.m.. This gave me just enough time to do a quick mineral, sulfa bath. We boarded the on-time bus and was greeted by Paul, a Maori chief and our host. On the ride to the Hangi Hakari, he gave us a brief, colorful history of what we were about to experience. I had this feeling that some of what he was telling us was for the benefit of the tourist.

At the sight we were ushered into the ceremonial house (Marae) and the performance began. The clear tones of the voices and the beat of the drums took me to a dream like consciousness. As I was watching the singers and dancers, a ray of bluish white light beamed like a spot light onto one of the women performers. She just glowed. I could not take my eyes off her.

After the ceremony, we were taken outdoors and shown how the special feast was prepared similar to the way it had been done in ancient times. While standing there watching and listening to Paul explain the rituals, the woman with the glow passed behind me on the way to her car. I knew I had to share the light experience with her. I walked a few feet to where she stood. I told her how beautiful the performance was and how I had seen the glow specifically around her. Being very modest and somewhat leery of a tourist, she told me she was still on the mend from having a cold and that this was her first night back. If I did not know then, I know now, there are no coincidences.

In the middle of our chat she pointed to the necklace I was wearing. She asked me where I had gotten it. I told her I had designed it and had it made. This did not satisfy her. She repeated, "Where did you get that?" Out of frustration for an answer I told her I channeled the design and had it made. At that moment she threw her arms around me and hugged me. She said something to the effect, "You are one of us."

After the hug, we were called to dinner. Yvonne, the still glowing woman, got into the car with her husband and went home. I went to dinner, but I could not get my mind off the experience I had just had. At dinner the chatter from the other guests bored me with their attempts to impress each other. It seemed so superficial compared to what I had felt only thirty minutes prior.

Also during the performance, I had received one of my past life mental movies. I knew I needed to ask Paul our guide some questions. I saw him sitting alone, drinking coffee, so I walked over and sat next to him. I asked if he would explain some of the images and symbols I had mentally received. I drew some of them on a napkin. He started giving me the "tourist 101" explanation. I stopped him in mid sentence and told him I wanted the real story. Before he could answer, he was summoned by one of his co-workers to take charge of the closing ceremonies.

After the ceremonies, we were ushered onto the bus that was to take us back to the motel. Bill and I sat toward the back. I still could not quit thinking about the mysterious events of the evening and about my unanswered questions.

As we were getting off the bus at our motel, Paul said to me, "We need to talk". I handed him my card with our room number on it.

The next morning I was up early doing my normal morning meditation and writing. About 7:30am I decided to go for a mineral bath. At this motel the mineral baths are in individual rooms. As I laid in the steaming water, I sensed the presence of several people's energy around me. I also sensed, intuitively, that I was being talked about.

About an hour and one half later, I went back to the room. Bill had just hung up the phone. He said, "You probably already know that Paul called. The Maori elders met and they want to meet your at 1:00 p.m.." I remember my only comment was, "Yes, let's get dressed and have breakfast."

One o'clock came and as prearranged we were picked up by Paul. He drove us to the home of the area chieftain, George and his wife, Tina. As the afternoon went on, we met quite a number of his family as they came and went. Among them was Rick, a tribal chief and his wife, Joslyn. At some point, Rick and Joslyn asked Bill and I if we would like to visit the Maori rain forest land the next day. We told them we would like that very much.

The next day Bill was feeling poorly, so I went with Rick and Joslyn alone. Rick had light hair and the brightest cobalt blue eyes. Most Maori have dark hair and dark eyes. Before going to the forest, they dropped their baby off at her mother's house. Upon meeting her mother, I had one of those "Nice to see you again" experiences, even though I had never met her. When we left for the rain forest Joslyn's mother gave me a big hug. Perplexed Joslyn made the comment that this was not her normal response to an American stranger.

After a beautiful morning in the rain forest, they brought me back to Joslyn's mother's house for lunch. Her mother and her step father had gone to the grocery store and were not back as yet, mainly because the visiting Queen of England had tied up traffic. The men, who were with us in the rain forest, had a meeting, so Joslyn, her sister-in-law, Yvonne and myself were left to have tea and chat. Joslyn asked about my recent trip to Peru and if I had seen any aliens. I told her about my experience at Lake Titicaca. She wanted to know what they looked like. I described them as seven and one half to eight feet tall, cobalt blue eyes and having six fingers. She nearly dropped her tea cup.

She then told me the story her mother-in-law had told her when Joslyn became pregnant with her first child. Rick, her husband had been born with six fingers. This "defect" was considered a bad omen, so his mother threw him in the corner and would not feed him. Rick's grandmother picked him up, took him to her home and did a spiritual ritual while she cut off his sixth finger. What all this means, I will let everyone make their own conclusions.

I will say this. Many of the Maori legends and some of their folklore suggest a land mass to the north where the teachers were not from the earth. Could these happy natives of New Zealand be descendants of the original people of Lemuria, the sunken continent in the Pacific?

If the warmth and friendliness of the Maori is any indication of what is may have been like at the time of Lemuria, let it rise again.

New Zealand
(Message on plane going to New Zealand)

There will be a chance to meet a chief
The encounter does not have to be brief

Take notes of what you see and hear
It will help you remember when you, before, were there

The symbols and colors will tell a story
Of the time when Lemuria was in her glory

Meditate by the sea at night
And we will give you quite a sight

Out to the sea your spirit will float
There will be no need for any kind of boat

On Lake Taupo you will feel a charge
From the energy that is very large

A comment from Claudette; On the plane trip to New Zealand I asked my spirit guides what to expect of my visit to this country below ;the equator.

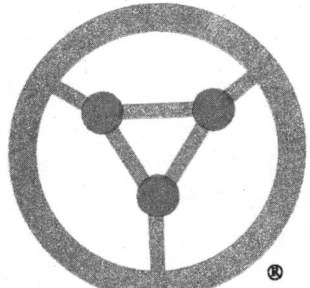

The necklace design that Yvonne asked about

Milarepa

Gary, our personal tour guide in Tibet, stood up on our bus and asked, "Since there is stormy weather moving in, how many of you want to see the cave of Milarepa?" Almost beyond my control, my hand shot up into the air along with enough other people's to warrant our stopping at the cave situated high in the Hymalayas. At the time my hand was in the air, my mind was asking, "Who is Milarepa?" I had no idea. I just knew I had to see that cave in the side of the cliff.

When the bus stopped, I saw a small village built on the side of a mountain at about 18,000 feet elevation. Those of us wanting to see the cave walked down a winding path, somewhat guarded by wandering yaks. We walked through the village, then down some stairs to the entrance of a monastery, inside of which was Milarepa's cave. We waited a while for a monk to come to unlock the gate. I could not conceive who would want to steal a cave.

When the gate was opened, I walked to the entrance of the cave and stepped inside. I found myself in a pitch black cave where Milarepa lived and meditated in solitude in the llth century AD. The cave probably measured less than six feet by eight feet and was about six feet in height. I was told Milarepa meditated in this cave as a hermit in order to achieve Nirvana for months at a time eating only soup made from thistles. Legend says this is the reason he is pictured with green skin.

When I came out of the cave, I walked to the edge of the cliff. Hundreds of feet below was a rapidly moving river with steep cliffs and mountains bordering both sides of it. As I stood gazing down, a bank of misty clouds came creeping up the river. All sound seemed to cease except for a barely audible sound of music. Even the roar of the swift mountain river slamming itself against the rocks as it journeyed to its final destination, seemed muted.

As this misty cloud came closer, it started rising as though it was coming directly toward the cave. The closer it came, the more certain I was, that the faint sound, I was hearing was singing and not the wind playing tricks on my mind. The tone of the voice was very soothing, almost hypnotizing. When the cloud finally engulfed me and the cave, I had no doubt that I was witness to a special spiritual event.

It was not until later that I learned that Milarepa, Tibet's greatest yogi, sang his often rhymed spiritual messages throughout the country. It, also, was not until later that I learned that many nomads, today, have also heard his songs while they traveled through the Tibetan terrain.

The poem "A tribute to Milarepa" expresses my gratitude for the spiritually altering experience I had on the side of that cliff. I believe there is a message in this rhymed poem for all of us. I have an innate feeling that Milarepa, himself, may have had a hand in writing the message.

Sing Your Song
(A Tribute To Milarepa, a Beloved Saint of Tibet)

Milarepa, my dear poet from the past,
You have learned "The Way", the die you did cast.

Why do you return to sing to us once more?
Are your songs different or are they the same as before?

Is it only a remembrance that causes our tears to flow
Or do you pierce our hearts with your words that glow?

Sometimes in your words, the true message we may miss,
But in the melody we feel your kiss.

Again and again you have sung of "The Way"
Please be patient when off the path we may stray.

The mountains continue to sing your songs of praise.
They remind us that even turmoil is, but a sacred phrase.

Oh great poet, sing your songs loud and clear,
For you see dear Mila, many of us are finally ready to hear

A comment from Claudette:

As this poetic tribute to Milarepa was being channeled through to me, I heard words from the Sesame Street theme song, "Sing a Song" in the background of my mind. The words, "Sing a song, don't worry that it's not good enough, just sing, sing a song" kept repeating.

The background serenade helped me to put my negative ego in its place and to let the words I was hearing just flow onto the paper. It helped me to recognize how very strong and sabotaging my negative ego can be if I allow him to take charge. From my higher self I say this. To the many Milarepas of the world, just sing your song. Sing it loud and clear.

The Himalayas
(Written immediately after experiencing Milarepa's cave)

What is the purpose, this travel to lands
Where the physical is tested and the ancient stands

Is it to remember who I was long in the past
And to be shown my true purpose for now at last

Why did I choose now to journey this far
Is there a reason or am I merely following a star?

The roads are bumpy, the food uneatable
But very seldom is my heart regrettable

When did I acquire a taste for yak butter tea
Or enjoy the sandalwood incense that permeates the air free.

The mountains, the glaciers, they are all here
But also the feeling of overwhelming fear.

Why must the spirit be taught only through fear and control.
Like an eagle it should fly free, its own soul to patrol.

We make a stop to watch the yak with their bells that ding dong
If we listen closely we hear the hills respond with a song.

We wind up narrow and rough mountain passes
Close to the edge we hear squeals from the lasses.

So barren and desolate the terrain does appear
Could God really have created this, with much care?

A lonely herder waves to us with a smile
For he know God is with him as he travels each mile.

We wonder how with the elements he can cope
But on his face we see only peace and hope.

Did we need to travel this far to understand
That peace comes from within no matter what the land.

Her Eyes,
The Window to Her Soul

High in the Himalayas in a little village in southern Tibet, our small bus pulled into a station for fuel. Our group of fifteen road worn seekers piled off the bus in search of cold drinks and bathroom facilities. An outhouse with ventilation was a real treat.

As had been the case at most of our stops, we were immediately surrounded by Tibetan children tanned by the intense mountain sun. Their tiny hands were outstretched begging for gifts or money.

Most of us had our cameras on us. Mine had become a permanent appendage. Everywhere we looked, there was beauty in one form or another. After standing there a few minutes, breathing in the magnificence of the surrounding snow capped Himalayas, I felt a strong but gentle energy directly behind me. When I turned the eyes of a tiny Tibetan woman met mine. For a moment I fully understood what it meant to be One with someone. As I took her picture, a broad smile formed on her face, telling me, we both understood who each other really was.

Even though her clothes were soiled and worn, I, not once, felt sorry for her. If anything I envied her, for she truly knew who she was. Our messengers come in all shapes and sizes and often when we least expect them. The poem that follows tells the lesson I learned.

A Tibetan Star

A face that has seen
Many a sunrise,
Her life full of toil
With not many a surprise.

But yet a smile
Shines upon her face.
The lines of life
A delicate lace,

Her hair has grayed
But not her soul,
It shines ever bright;
It has paid the toll.

Eyes that have seen much
Still shine ever bright
Ever filled with hope
For they see the Light.

She meets the stranger
With her small cupped hand,
Although always begging,
Proud she does stand.

Her attire is simple;
It protects from the cold,
What hidden gems
Does she conceal in each fold.

A Tibetan Star

I feel no pity
For her path is her choice,
I judge not her path
For we hear the same voice.

The Lotus

The Lotus Flower (padma)
As the flower rises from muddy roots, so Nivana arises from this shabby world and thus it symbolizes purity.
The power to open its petals comes from the core of the lotus bloom. If pulled open by someone else, the petal withers and dies, for it has not as yet gained the courage, strength and wisdom through its veins that only its core can send.

Bamboo

Often flutes and other musical instruments are made from the stalks of the Bamboo plant. The wind sways its limber stalks and as they touch one another , they create beautiful musical tones and harmonies.

Golden Silence

*The silence is golden
If you make it so.
Then everything you touch
Will take a glow.*

*If you fear
What your eyes can not see,
Open your eyes
And at peace you will be.*

*Nothing or everything
Will be new to you.
Remembering, is the force
That will cook the stew.*

*Each ingredient
Is an intricate part.
As they become One,
Results in a whole, that is smart.*

The Silent Place

Hear the snowflake
Hit the ground,
Cover your ears
For so loud the sound,

Such a roar
The humming bird's wings do make.
Can not those petals
Be more quiet for peace's sake?

This is not silence
As I have been told,
The deeper I go
The warmer the cold,

My ears are afire
In this silent place,
If I go deeper
Would there be, also, noise in space?

In this deep, silent place
A new orchestra does play
The harmonious songs say
I have found "The Way".

The Sea and Thee

The roll of the wave
Is the way we behave

It comes in with a splash
It goes out with no clash

It is clear I can see
Until it picks up debris

It deposits its baggage
On the shore with a ravage

The spray that it showers
Opens my inner flowers

As I watch the waves bend
I see, no beginning, no end.

No Beginning, No End

Whenever, I had asked, during meditation, for guidance on how to begin this book of stories and rhymed messages, the phrase "There is no beginning and no end", would come through to me loud and clear. My human frustration clouded the true meaning of this phrase for many years. It was not until I let go of my ego's control of me and went to that deep silent place within me was I clear of its significance.

Spiritually, the essence or soul never dies. The container it is in may change, but that God energy, the soul, is forever, never ending therefore, never beginning. It is infinite. Like nature has shown me repeatedly, energy constantly changes and transforms, a never ending circle of events.

One of my students insisted that I mention the fact that crystals continue to grow and change physically, as well as spiritual. We, human souls, are not much different from the crystals or other creations.

This book also illustrates the never ending concept. Even though it has a page one, the reader can begin reading on any page and still experience the message intended for him. This book is presented to you as a living, growing and constantly changing being. It has been my experience and maybe that of yours, that every time I read one of these channeled rhymed messages, I acquire a different meaning. Whatever my quandary is at that moment the message seems to give me the insight to answer the question I am searching.

My spiritual board of directors and I suggest that you use this book as a spiritual fertilizer, not unlike the brand name, "Miracle Grow", is to plants. Even after completely reading this book, occasionally open it and read the message written on that page. It may just be the stimulant your spirit needs to rise out of its stagnation at that moment. Always remember, it is an open invitation to come "Fly With Me"

The End and The Beginning

A Comment from the Human Author

I think this book is beautiful, but what mother does not think her baby is beautiful. Enjoy.

Claudette

About The Author

Claudette Cleveland is an artist and a writer who considers the world her home.

She shares her vast spiritual knowledge and experiences through her seminars and lectures. As a hypnotherapist and healer Claudette has seen results that could be termed "miraculous".

For years she has shared her spiritual quests through her art and the spoken word. Now, she has chosen the written word in the form of a book as her medium in which to express the trials and turmoils as well as the hopes and joys of her spiritual journey.

Claudette is a Reiki Master, a member of the National Hypnotherapists Guild and a member of the International Society for Poets

Her paintings are shown through out the world. Her poetry and stories have been published in many periodicals. "The Peace We Knew" published by The National Library of Poetry contains one of her poems. This is the first book of many that Claudette plans to publish.